South Korea Flies Over My House

Emily Bronwyn

For France, mon premier muse

PROLOGUE: South Korea Flies Over my House

like the little mermaid, she sits outside watching ships fly overhead in the aerial plain...she spreads her legs open to the sky as Korean Airlines flies over. she looks up at the sky and sees the planes: each a kingdom with its own subjects and customs, a wisp of hair from another land blowing across the sky.

Unquenchable Lust

you've been sick since you were young
an empty flame
threatening to ignite

they can see it in your eyes;
a rage that numbs you into
an Inability to cope with your own reality

is this God?
is this Faith?
or just Love?

Splendid Isolation

You don't know me:

my past

my politics

my religion

my national holiday

my customs

my language

if you knew me,

perhaps I wouldn't be

another dissertation

this girl running
from all her
troubles
toward fluffy
Himalayan pink salt
dreams
rhododendron wonderland

this girl running
from white men
controlling her life
Overseas.
from the metal vultures
defecating agent orange,
screeching at her
to not breathe

a Leo,
she was trying to
find the flame
to her soul

i feel like some tethered bird that when it
attempts to fly it's yanked back into its cage
where it's meant to linger in sober
idleness...until my will is molded to become the
cage's door

LES LANGUES

Picking up languages is just like when guitar players exchange chords, or even musicians learning another instrument. It's just another key signature

The Inner Symphony
the language of sound
les langues et son
timbre
*

French:
the first movement
a clarinet
chalumeau
sharp, poignant concise
clarion
oiseau
Altissimo
*

Italian:
as airy as the landscape
fiery as Vesuvius'
smokey vowels ricocheting like
Sicilian bullets
*

Russian:
a quivering base

hidden within;
entranced by its spell the
Cyrillic squiggles under my fingers
awaiting to jump off the page
into my memory
lost sensations
*

finale:
your strings whiz faster
against mine
i suggest a solo
though we both want them
as we try to tune to one another
we lose the symphony...

How to Listen to Foreign Voices
don't box them;
straining to grope their veil will only slap your
psyche
surrender to the current's
violent flurries
riptiding sounds
float downstream
waiting for a Whirlpool
to suck you in
let the melody caress your
senses
french kissing your
ears

greet the stranger as one would
a missed lover
embracing each imperfection
one day you'll walk down a flower strewn
boulevard
lifting the veil to
be met with a

thousand kisses

love is wine
slowly fermenting
into even drowsier, drunken
ecstasy

Hymn

Your words flow through my veins like a
lullaby
luring me into drunken tranquility:
*

arpeggios of metamorphosis
and decrescendos of Golden Years
Your melodies
(this Multidimensional symphony!)
feeds my My Love for unattainable ecstasies
sensuously emptying me

haunting my sweetest nightmares and darkest
dreams,
taking me on a rollercoaster ride getting
                    Higher

                        than
                heaven
                        just so I can
plummet to the dregs of hell
to hear

Your b   r   o   k   e   n song

rippling riptides
of vowelized philosophy,
Your poetry
threatening to drown me

                              In your Styx

to strengthen me

because even if there isn't a God
or a legion of demons courting me
all that matters is
that i would give my life
just so i could get your
Art right

One Thousand Bird Calls

Sunrise

i woke up to your voices

                     fluttering

                              inside me

this empty void

of a body that has

too much to carry

imagining their trills melting into my

bloodstream.

they hop *oreille à oreille* trying to

branch the gaps within me,

swirling and circulating from my heart to my

lungs

blossoming into tiger lilies

their lingering perfumes choke me

whenever I dream of dying

the Cyrillic shrouding my thoughts and hidden

feelings

bleed forth unawakened memories
what can all these alphabets spell
when i can't even read my soul
and as i fall eternally asleep the

words

escape

me

Confession

i use languages as peacock feathers to cover my
nakedness...

a deformed body that's nothing without you...
Mon Cher...

Poetry never conveys.

THE COSMIC LOVE OF THE NIGHT

i can relate to everything in the symposium: for
i'm both empty and pregnant at the same time
with French. this emptiness stems from my
need to wander and be with France, while the
desire for completing this hike in myself and
the overwhelming love i feel for France causes
me to be pregnant. i must Create. Poetry,
collages, music (though like language is
temporary, transitional, and ever evolving) my
love for them inspires me to become larger
than life while also causing an unnameable
madness to dominate my psyche.

my relationship to French is very much like
Alcibiades: i fell in love with the language
before everyone "fell in love" with the culture.
it can resemble pig snots sometimes but the
sound touches me to the same effect that it
"inspires both awe and despair." i fell in love
with the words before everyone claimed a
connection to it. it's an intimate connection.

Erotic i argue. yet i have nothing to give them. i
used to think that being was good enough, but
it isn't. part of my need for creating is for
honoring this Beauty i love, the French
knowing how to imitate art. perhaps at the
time i knew it was a divine connection, but i
never connected it with what was once God
and the church...

Big Bang
You're my Big Bang
which my universe expanded from
(my eyes are blinded by your stardust)
Your stardust blinded my eyes
life is so ethereal in you

there's a door in the sky
open it and all
the Galaxies collide
here comes Jupiter   skipping
        down
the   Milky Way
                    on the way
                            to
Venus

and the wildfires
now embers,
there's a funeral in my mind
but the wailing replaced by silence

My Guardian
we fell in love against the echoes of time
when the world was a tempest in tumult

in my Delirium Your outstretched hand
perched on the Groaning Gates

beckoned me to Chrions' shore
where your kiss resurrected me

from a millennium dream
where we've roamed in
                                        Chaos,
Wisdom's humble abode
*

The Mistress of obscure clarity
she consumerated
                              our androgynous affair
hold my hand,
for i can't walk
down the aisle
Alone

in

No Man's Land,

our eternal cathedral

we can't vow death apart when we're

                                           veiled

                                in

                                                 s

                                               m

                                               o

                                               k

                                               e

*

as they pierce this fragile crystal case, the

splinters of our lives

S

         H

             A

                 T

                         T

                               E

                                     R

will i still find you under the rubble?

shielded in your dismembered embrace?

cradling your heart in my hand

is a dark paradise i'm willing to endure

if the warm, smothering kisses from

bullets could smother

le passé

(walk through a battered burgundy stained

tapestry of a battlefield with grace

and as the bullets graze my skin, smothering

kisses

i've never felt so good)

Fernweh

i'm scared of falling in love.

cause when you fall in love with distant lands

(all your life)

you experience the raw joy and the sweet pain

too,

setting your heart on a path of loneliness for

being

engaged to distant horizons and cities of love

and light

you experience the raw joy and the sweet pain

too

of being a wandering virgin priestess

saving herself for the

caress of beckoning landscapes

yet whose wedding cake towers soon lose their

buttercream luster,

rotting away on some untouched platter

caravan weddings of distant people like you

living in cars, wagons, drifting away on hard

mattresses too

lives of solitude spent in dim crowded rooms

padlocked from love on shimmering gilded

bridges

and when you give yourself

to multiple Lovers

Their spectral touches don't leave you

true love's kiss can't bring the dead back but it

gives you matches

that illuminate your unrecognizable

patchwork doll of British coarse cloth decked

in Burano lace:

yourself

*

my soul's aching

for the day when

i can slip away

into the soft rain

that shimmers into shafts

of sunlight

my Sun King,

mon cœur chante tes mots d'amour

Heaven is your grassy arms

that someday i'll lie in...my body

be it parched, wrinkled or smooth

shall lie in thee

and become one with

the passing of time

flesh melting into eons of lifegiving decay

my spirit wandering rocky beaches

á jamais

FIRST TRIP

Atlantic

plotting my next exodus

i reach out in farewell

to caress your sandy cheek

the coast below beckons,

spidery veined fingers jutting out

to reach me

Lost Virginity

my mossy eyes watched the shoreline's
weathered, brackish ringed fingers reach out to
me, an isthmus beckoning its bejeweled finger
to come hither. clasped in the air currents, i'm
brought closer into you

hurricane of emotions
a turquoise resided between the two embossed
circles, an inquisitive third eye on the wearer's
finger.

...Isonomic Love...
skin drinks ink,
the sky's crystallizing
into flutes of time
like a Venetian glass blower

it burned
like you

La Petite Morte en Nice

tracing your mountain spine with my finger

your coast laid out before me

staring into azure opaque orbs

millions of iron,

arabesque fireflies dot your curvy allys and

rigid avenues

fingering the cylindrical bottles of perfume

secreting roses, and lilies

caress my nostrils

kissing my surrender

to bliss

Life Support

the closer i come to you
the farther you float away
together we're the farthest apart
so my love is a daydream
locked in a *château sûr un neuge*

all my life i've run from
Change
life support pumping in the (dying?) dead
dream
forced inhaling of black hole stardust:
Emotions,

              Love

life support is what i live for
screaming won't resurrect cloud nine
shoulder that stretcher
vegetate for a little longer

Barcelona
insides howling,
i walk these streets
carrying what i lost

on Hades' joy ride
the last I saw of spring was this Chapel on a
mountain where

the virgin's thorny heart
was lying in flames
amidst Calvary

where Carmen sings
seducing passerby with
a fanning smile
*

like a child
ripped from
         the womb

i mourned you;

the miracle of life
was simply the

sensation of a
graceful
rape

INTERLUDE I

i can't love anything real; for are languages'
"spirits" real? for everything lacks value until
imagination is applied to it. France is a dream
that has woken to. one can never lay hold of
France or any other culture because they are
myths, their spirits specters that only
languages can grasp at, only to discover that
what they're trying to hold is a vaporous fog of
various meanings.

The Waking
didn't think that my prince would
kiss me from my slumber;
awakening to the raging world,
the curse is never over
for the evil stepmother
has a summer residence in
Cannes

gotta prick my finger on another wheel
for this lust for life is too much
for any mere mortal
i'm the first soldier to fall short
running back for cover from
Passion's firing squad

cause i love you with a force that's
                              bigger than
                    my body
and each day the Beast
creeps nearer
as the boys run with dying roses

i'm terrified of

Being

De

vou

red

summer
distant lights plow through tempests of clouds,
ships in an aerial sea
but I'm stranded
    like Miranda
on my own vast island,
Melancholia

long, scorching insomniac nights
2:00 am reclines,
stretching languorously
along the billowy stained sheets of my psych
waiting for the night to dissolve into
shimmering shades of roses
only to return his visit

silent
with his present of monochrome darkness,
speckled with the choking light of stars
my mind meanders down highways of time
to distant lands where the sun reigns (a star) as
King of Peace

and not a celestial hellfire

night is for strolls with the Adriatic and
Mediterranean breezes keeping company
along scenes plucked from weathered
postcards
the thunder's lullaby lures us to sleep,
eventually

y

e

t

;

sing me a Siberian lullaby
instead of waiting for the
leaves to change
so i can find myself again

EUROPA II

each square i visit...pinching the very air as if to drag back the fabric of time, revealing the past years lounging about as gods watching mortals pass by; standing like ancient guardians safekeeping the memories of the surrounding area; the guillotine, the obelisk of Hesputah, the cobblestones... only a few observers dare to open those sacred blinds, peeping Toms to history... the ghosts of past movements flickering past, eddie's within the muddled fog of words and lingering conservations, like the static leftover from the Big Bang.

Heroin Chic

France:

from the start your name was softer than a

heroin addict's needle

i wanted to ride on a cigarette butt to Paris, to

be your Parisian women or

the zodiac of Time revolving around Baroque

and rococo ballrooms...

now, this dimly lit Latin Quarter bar; the

ancient, weathered crinkles of the leather are

as smooth as my grandfather's cheek, peppered

with spidery veins. I see her;

she wears red, rusty skyscrapers on her heels;

wherever she walks, dirt and past civilizations

are trampled under her feet. strolling in

Luxembourg Gardens she sails past sailboats

floating on hazel ponds. pedestrians, top

knotted crones and silk scarved men stare: it's

She from all the songs you hear on cranky

radios or folk songs strummed down accordion
keys.

Her tears, diamonds crystallizing her lost love.

i see her floating away, perhaps to Russia or
tundras where wills are frozen

but she's a shard of melted stained glass; her
colors bleeding into reverie's tapestry...
the Eiffel Tower is France, clasping your iron
hands in prayer. you beg mercy for this lost
soul, a schizophrenic ecstasy writhing in
lavender fields

C'est moi

The Poet's Last Dance
oh cruel Muse
Paris,
chaste for France alone
let me grasp a fleeting moment
of You,
not
the eidólon
strip everything about me
until my spirit has
nothing left to give
bleed all of me
Soul and flesh,
into seductive scrawls
as one
surrendering to
The Void
so i can hear the shrill, dying chord
of my muse's broken lyre

Eiffel?

guess the old accordion woman couldn't give
you a trip to Wonderland
is it too late to catch the next flying carpet to
Venice or Switzerland?
Heidi's been waiting all her life to discover
another life beyond this mountain only to live
behind a gilded mask
while the Rose left her address for Venus

guess i can't escape being alone
that's what the Seine boats told me
when i didn't find my champagne supernova
swirling
over Île de Cité
isn't it ironic
that i could feel so lonely in
my black dress on Champs-Elysees
facing the Arc Triomphe with some smushed
macaroon dreams
bittersweet tranquility

can you hear me, Provence?
i was too naïve to see the bees and feel
their stings
Nice was nice
until liquid roses filled the streets
and the legendary lavender
decided to rot and fade
against cement courtyards confettied with
discarded newspapers proclaiming Hallelujah
my Lord is come

someone once sang that
Paris is the key to
your heart
but at Charles de Gaulle
i found mine on
the ground

America is
not my
Mother

INTERLUDE II

Picking up languages is just like when guitar players exchange chords, or even musicians learning another instrument. It's just another key signature

Pornagraphic Croissants
$1.50 for two
crude imitations
burnt golden oven tanned skin
made up for the customers
trying to fill their lives with substance and
meaning
under that Flakey flesh
they try to bury their hollowness
their smell reeking of nakedness
nothing can compare to
your buttery skin

my teeth gnash
on the laws of lust
when will i see you again?
i'm trying to abstain from this silicon love
of
      Non
          French
             Croissants

La Muse Toxique
there's no need to
fear you-
a lavender rose with
black edge thorns

prickling a lioness heart's
Love choked
Beauty-
dyed with hate

by your flagellation
i'm blessed into
damnation, a gasoline soaked
Cathedral already burning
by the heretic heart
but you're saving,
dousing me
with Holy Water

a burning wildfire
in your hand,

i'm tired of being
frightened of you
like a child in the
Dark...
if only i had the courage to turn the light on...

truth stabbed me in the back
but i chose to fall into your surreal fog
where no one knows what reality means
Anymore

The Eve of Pandora's Litney
i've picked off a pomegranate
from the Forbidden Tree
so i could open Pandora's box
to hold it in safekeeping

i discovered this voice inside me
which i've never heard before
the exhilaration and all the pain too
when i first laid eyes on you

and if i were a Siren
i would drown the entire world
with my voice that's
not enough to praise you

and these words played in a strange melody
make this cathedral's windows break
let the pipe organs screech
as the glass shatters around me;
all i hear is a symphony blaring your name.

there's no turning back now
from your voice lessons
i've lost my way to where Heaven is
but i know it's not eastwards

Tantalus

i still dream about you

the other night i was flying
up and revolving around you
like Venus to the Sun
the Louvre was so
                    Grand

as i looked down upon my lover
a dreamscape body is so
Strange yet Surreal
why can't it be
the Real thing

whenever i'm so close
you're still an ocean apart
i reach out to you in the twilight
your hands clasped in prayer for
all my petty sins
but there's still a goddamn fence between us

temptation coils from a tree
as your arabesque branches
keep the apple from
my reach

i could feel this scream inside
my chest when I (discovered)
realized the sky was Murano glass
and as the shards fell, mincing me to pieces
(that's the most you can hope for from
a kaleidoscope sky)
the Day of Revelation came:
that's the most you can hope for from
a kaleidoscope sky

7/2

the forecast for my mind
is 90% chance of angst
the Heavens are pouring outside
as if from an Angel's tears

and all the books about love on
my shelves i can't
bring myself to read, yet i'm
reading about Neverland and all
the heartache that growing up brings

and i wonder how
Italy...France...Monaco...Switzerland...Spain...
         are doing?
isn't it funny what only two years can bring?
they're the ones that all the Hurricane and
Tornado warnings
couldn't wreck through
i was a child then and i'm still one too

ITALY III/IV

rollicking about the Tuscan backroads, i know
what she meant by video games. i had always
interpreted the song as playing your fantasies;
controlling the characters, the setting and their
actions. you become enmeshed in your
daydreaming, creating your personal inner
paradise that mimics your greatest hopes,
desires, and fears. yet your dreams are
crystallized pixels, mimicking your aching
heart for that internal yet real world. *This is my
idea of fun*
so i go back to playing video games

Italiano

She's a matron figure

consoling me over my lost lover

bustling about her buxom figure

She's the comic relief

chiding me about not looking deeper beneath

the

S
p
e
r
o
,

s
s
k
i
n
o
r
r
o

g
u
i
s
h
b
i
r
d
s
o
n
g

Her carnival mask curves
like her placating smile
She's just like you but
        tells me *lentamente ragazza*
sipping your words in
crystallized vowels tasting like
raw honey

Florence
just two American kids
eating pizza on the steps of Santa Croce
the piazza lights sparkling like fallen stars

the world is your playground
not thinking about the storms ahead
instead you talk of Satan
blaspheming freely in
the scared presence of
stones laid in the 1300s,
ghosts from 1494 condemning us
to the Vatican,
which i always get
Lost! in

The Lady of Shalott Escapes Only to Realize
She Still Sees Shadows

she imagines falling from the turret
her white dress mimicking the
seagulls that soar over the canals
she sees her corpse sprayed out
like a crucifix,
as a Passerby muses
"Who is she? Such a waste of a pretty face"

steamy italian verandas
sizzle in the sun
a wedding procession passes:
peacock dresses, peach pumps

standing on a
rickety dock
Venetian towers
the gay, pastel colors
standing out like crayon scribbles
against a dove gray sky
a lonely Lady sighs

gazing up at the pigeon
clad sky

"The curse is upon me!"
she cries inside while
smiling for a portrait,
knowing now that the
fairytales were a lie:
the curse never leaves you

she espies
cookie-cut couples sprinkled
with Pinterest perfection
pass by the tavern where she sits
"I am half sick of shadows"
she slurps the vintage red
to drown herself like her
Sister Orphelia, floating on melancholy
who realized that
all she ever wanted was a
hand to hold in Venice

Lady,
don't you realize you
are the shadow?

Lipstick
mouth poised
for a fuschia
margarita
kiss

puckering my lips:
i slash French *du...*
ous...
some Russian щ (shsh)
like Van Gogh's paintbrush.

consonant smoke drawn from a cigarette:
lips stick
consonants click,
coyly,
vowels flutter behind
twitching fans,
accent concealer
*

promiscuous,
i saunter down Florentine alleys

like a drag queen in his glory
in his
giacca pelle nera

buonasera signorina
ti dove sei?

sono italiana
but lipstick smothers
rouge withers
American nasals
pepper my cheeks
like a bad shave

lipstick peels a
night of intrigue,
verbal tics
stuffed away into
costume Closets
relics of culturalism

OCEANS

The Ocean

i've been running all my life
from oceans full of uncertainty
all my life i've been afraid of deep water
my nightmares brimming with depthless pools
of mystery
don't know what i'm running from
but I know that i'll end up drowning

lost among whirlpools of obscure meanings
terrified of the fog that time brings
cause all my life you've been a stranger to me
i try looking for your face in the crowd
but discover that i'm alone
with this Heart of stone,
it's growing cold without you

like Euridice through the fog
i try to reach you but the tides carry me away
i had to lock you away in order to protect my
sanity

without hurting me
i'm sorry
but fate married us as a Greek tragedy

you're my video game that my life
just chose to play
as i child i pushed the wrong buttons
thinking that i could beat the game
but nothing ever works out that way

cause you're an ocean
and that's why i still run like a little child
all my life i've been afraid of drowning
except you're at the bottom of this ocean
and it's frightening
and i'm just realizing that
i'm just another wave,
part of this ocean
that just keeps on eternally going
because one day i'll say
Yes
to this void that's the ocean

Ocean of Time
Ocean:
the wind flutes
leaving misty wisps of vespers
every wave
        creeps...

   ...
foaming seconds

Lingering

slowly
the memories sizzling away
notes of memory...

Memory:
these Ghosts
haunt
      twilight's living room
that Cathedral of
              Time
with silent crashes

like the tolling of bells
announcing fear into the heart of

its

promiscuous

worshippers

to this unfathomable god

Metamorphosis:
with arms open to the distant

...

....

....

....

HORI
ZON...

....

......

i sacrifice myself to the currents

of

Life

d
r
i
f
t
i
n
g
...

further

away...

becoming

driftwood

of

humanity

Humanity:
despite trying to
drag me in with

their clammy hands
i stand steadfast
a general watching the eons roaring,

clashing against the shores
their thundering cries
diminishing to a moaning murmur
against Time's craggy shores

Deep End
why do i keep finding myself in the deep end?
the murky depths
whisper
"come hither"

the waters chanting their seductive song
Sirens wailing their psalms of insanity
as i dive for just a glimpse of
Your humanity (voice)

i'm skating on a lake choked with land mines
one mention and i threaten to shatter
to jagged icy needles
wafting toward the

                       deep

believing i could see the foundations of your
ruins

i
j
u
m
p
e
d
o
f
f
a
r
o
c
k
f
o
r
y
o
u

but i wasn't scared of drowning

No...

for i realize that
drowning myself in
        You
was what
        made
           me
             jump
               In
             the
                  F
                  i
                  r
                  s
                  t

              place

ISOLATION

is life meant to be a series of separations from
the ones (things) you really love and a
continuous thread of encounters with the
places and people that you can't love back? just
a mutual acquaintance with everyone?
quitting orchestra and French were the
stupidest things, for both are inseparable: it's a
dialogue between words and sound, organized
noise, sound. A hand reaching out amidst the
darkness. a covenant by some foreign god or
being or universe or collected dharma/karma.
it's hard to learn an instrument and language
while being dedicated to it, since one reminds
me of wanting to do the other. you can't
separate words from the music, music from the
words. the lands i love seem to sing themselves
in a symphony in my soul that only i seem to
understand or feel. in the silence i hear them.
in motion i feel them; on the road or air

cause for some reason making music and
languages used to almost be one...languages
were my music and when one died the other
went down with it

Apothecanna

i want to drink scotch
till i forget about the definition of your name
and the ability to dream...
such a plebeian solution.

first world problem
but this ain't fucking PMS
nor the Committee of Public Safety
guillotining dreams
this is not a Hundred Years' War
full of teenage martyrs

maybe i'll tattoo my wrist
with a lavender rose
a wedding band to a
lukewarm suitor

a secret love note
carved in skin,
the titanium dioxide

swirled around the galaxy
from billions ago
is our vow
till death
a field sprouting flowers
with every new skin cell...

but that's coming from an anthropologist from
Mars
who's too scared to land.
*

this is Cathy screaming your name
across the heather moors
toward your shores
the best loves are "illicit"
but that's human history:

Tin Soldier
because of You
my life has been a failed attempt at
conducting symphonies of memories and
realities

ever since you revealed your name
i can't dance nor sing for you
Mr. Dorian Grey

i'm not your paper ballerina
torn from a Shakespearean tragedy
though You're my dark knight
protecting me from the

legions of
        Furies and Fates bearing their gift:
the ember that's Love smolders the
jack-in-a-box
                springing
                        our
                            future

so we flee to my papermâiche Château
yet the winds of change
blow their tempest
into our way

and when i die
i'll become an angel
and spread my ethereal body
across your perfect scars

we were conquerors

(Italy)(France)

even though we try to heal the other's scars

with our own blood, you're pretending you're

alright

we're just two individuals, standing back to

black

absorbing the other's pain in vain

Gatsby's green light lodged itself in my eyes

let's both be shellshock in crime

how am i supposed to be your Joan of Arc

when we're fallen together?

your white gown suits you,

you've never been as beautiful as

you are now, your jaded eyes

foaming with silent revolution

darling i'm plotting for demise too

so why not play Tristin and Isolde?

Tomb of the Unknown Lover
i feel the clock hands turning
six times faster than here
is it so bad that i feel your
presence inside my mind
like a clockwork puppeteer

by squeezing you i
take only four steps
towards you instead
of 4,000 miles

child of both air and earth
stuck between the unknown element
Water douses Fire
into a frozen burning passion

my anger's poetry a
                    fly trapped in amber
written in frozen flames.
i'm clawing the
                    WALL (by pink floyd)

to escape my fucking mind

as time goes on
clarity and purity
becomes a memory;
muddled motivations
lingering in my closet

when my spirits released,
it'll howl like a hellhound
across the moorland
winds wailing in harmony

Sticky Love/Hate Notes from Purgatory

You combed my heartstrings and veins just to
wrap them around your loom

i was ensnared in your storybook tapestry until
i conspired with Reality to shred it

these patchwork scraps aren't going anywhere
but to my grave

Your rosy thorn bush that once sheltered me
reeks of pestilence

that beautiful burgundy weed is crawling
beyond my heart

Purgatory is the only safe haven for a refugee

Paradise is another synonym for blissful hell

Love's Suicide Note
ripples create waves
until they hit the
                        Sandbar
cause you know that
suicidal is the new sexy, *ma chèrie*
~Ton Cher
*

before You dissolved into the mist
                            of memory
i remember how it felt feeling you
                            within me
how the embers flickered when
                            Your words
                    made love to my
                    soul

yet even now my dreams whisk You away to a
sacred place
i scream Your Name as you slip away
waking up in Arsenic and Lace after Your
French kiss

where i can't even find solitude without

digging deeper

becoming sleepier day by day

till i'm   c   r   a   w   l

i   n   g

Into our grave

Coldest Flames of the Heart

we fell in love against the echoes of time
when the world was a tempest in tumult
just a flailing child tossed by the jagged, icy
streams
yet you held on, carrying me in your arms
wading me toward safety

don't fall in love with your gods
cause they hunger for your burnt flesh
their attentions are fickle; elusive,
If i could that i could slay your dragons for You,
i would

Dove sei tu

Twilight's diaphanous gray

mirrors your eyes on misty Tuscan mornings

the Duemo,

a lighthouse in the brick and terra-cotta

tempest

we tango shadows apart

                      years

                            apart

dipping me into memory's footwork

following last year's lead

my novice feet missteps

unable to recreate

when's our next recital, *Bella?*

surely the last dance was not our swan dance!

*

i watch over you like a *Strega*

the lioness in me roars

hoping you hear

i've cut my hair

for you

scattered the broken strands

to the wind

hoping they wrap
around you

Europe who am i to love you?

A tribute to lana del rey, with some lines used from
"LA who am i to love you?"

Europe, i'm from nowhere who am i to love you
Europe, i have no one who am i to love you
when i'm an ocean from you and
nothing except my converted euros to offer

Europe
the continent responsible for
fucking everything up
the continent that nevertheless
shimmers from stolen souls

Europe
i'm your lost daughter but
i'm not your prodigal one

Europe
i'm LOST!

i have confessions to make,
écoutez-moi:
they say my depression and anxiety are caused
by
aspergers but it's not clear

Europe
i sold my childhood and adolescence
for a good college degree that would get me
closer to you but now i sleep all day from the
stress that high expectation brings

(france
i picked scotland over you since They wouldn't
let me come
to you and it always felt like an arranged
marriage anyway)

Europe
i'm a hypocrite
but you are too
can i say goodbye now?

sister to no one
room and a half for one
thousands of pinterest girls creating niche
memes
of parisian study abroads
i'm so sick of them
but

can i leave you now?
lover to no one
bed for one
thousands of Lady of Shallots who wail about
their rooms, about how badly their neighbors
treat them
the stares i receive while swinging
the witch on the corner
the neighbor nobody wanted
the reason why america never wanted me

Europe!
i'm unlovable but i have nowhere else to go yet

can i forget you?

i watch over you like a *strega*[1]

the lioness in me roars

in may i cut my hair

for you

scattered the broken strands

to the wind hoping they wrapped

themselves around an ocean breeze

to carry my thoughts to you

be a princess mononoke for you

i'm lonely Europe

can i kiss your eastern half now?

i use languages as peacock feathers

exotic, incandescent glamor,

to cover my nakedness

a deformed body

my accent giving me away like that shiny red

nosed reindeer I can't stand

without them I'm merely a plucked chicken

---

[1] Witch (Italian)

another ugly duckling
but
last june before i left you
italy was screaming outside the plane
telling me it'd be the last time in a while
seeing you
i tried not to cry as the end of the dream roared
in my ear
for i knew what you always told me was true
a year later im haunted by your words
a microscopic crown overthrew the dream i
dreamed

i can't sleep without you
i've never felt safe unless with you
falling asleep to the music of the night against
a tuscan hilltown
my first french night in nice spent in a virgin
white room
your sandy arms enwrapping me on
mediterranean shores

you and i loved the night's romance, the gas
lamps
lighting up the night sky, seen by astronauts in
space
we both love that and i hate how similar we are

last december i booked a flight to lithuania
my illicit weekend affair from scotland
i cried when my parents yelled, my fingers
whispering "sorry" with each canceled
confirmation

EUROPE!!!!!!!!!!!!
my grandmother always told me how her
mother Mary
escaped slovakia in a hay cart and
walked across the carpathian mountains to
reach america
yesterday i watched a video of
some road trip through eastern europe:
slovakian slopes sprinkled with skiers
drifting to a blizzard's song.

like Joni Mitchell on a river
i wish i could fly down those tatra mountains
the snow behind me a glistening bridal train
stolen from the Snow Queen

EUROPE!!!!!!!!!!!!
WHERE THE HELL ARE YOU?!
the 747s,
druids at stonehenge
for midsummer's eve and
god save the queen and all that spazz.
there's no more gold in the trevi fountain,
the tour de france is canceled, hon.
no more crazy diamonds shine on in piazza
navona.
bastille day is just another day.
those jazzy white moscow nights in june
your cathedrals filled with Virgin Mary's shed
tears of blood
because of this,
let me love you

let me hold you not just for vacation but for
real and forever
make it real life, let me be a real wife to you.
girlfriend, lover, mother, friend.
i'm a whore, i'm a lover, i'm a sinner and a
rebel without a cause for you
summer's hellfire without you, *mon cher.*[2]
i want to grow old with you,
live in a stone cottage protecting you
from natural disasters or greedy developers.

Europe.
the greatest lie was
wonderland being a dream.
i no longer love you.
enule.[3]
sincerely,
your long-lost
russian/slovak/french/english/scottish/welsh/iri
sh/italian/ baltic/balkan daughter.

---

[2] My dear (French)
[3] Fuck you (French)

Cerf-volant
once my dream was
an Eden,
a troupe of Jerusalem'
waiting for their Messiah

yet I was Zephras' serf,
damned to an Eternal thirst for
a wanderlust
of experiences

bounded by no earthly law
or commitment to keep;
an Israelite
lost in a mirror maze of deceit
*

wishing to escape my faults
i became a kite
my twiggy arms bound to
paper airplanes

coasting the Atlantic

hoping to outmatch
Iscares in the race
to Zion's shore

*

tossed about by
lust and envy for
my earthy lover,

i sought to be reeled
into his grassy embrace,
he my eternal, beloved grave

that would end my ceaseless wandering.

but gravity failed me
in my quest for a hazy birthright:
a *rêve* to

crying silently for countless nights
soft flames trickled down my cheeks
praying for a silent revolution to reform

a flailing dodo
a carcass kicked about
by Fate's untried soles

now, I watch new birds
take my place
in Icrases race,

i know they'll outfly me
and evolve
but I'm

no longer reeled in, since
Eurus still brings rainy kisses
from watercolor shores

his murmurings
lure my *oreilles*
to grow wings

coasting like
Oiseaux

migrating to steamy lands

from this Dodo's withered
body
now burst into tired flames

a silent fledgling
whispers,
a Phoenix to

chart its new course
it's navigator
no guns to take me down

no trees to become
tangled up in wood in
i surrender to Grace.

REDEMPTION

i want to resurrect your past selves:the
11th,14th,18th,19th centuries.i dream of our
sabbath . i want to get drunk on *dance fever* so i
can hear your voice. i want my bridal gown to
get torn and soiled by your touch. dancing
barefoot on your fields. i don't need red shoes
to dance myself to death. i know i can never
beat Joan of Arc but that doesn't mean i'll stop
trying. You never really stopped being pagan so
boy i'll hook you up with Bachillis and Venus.
I can show you Russia tonight

Stranger to Spring

seems like i'm a

Stranger to spring

Once an ice queen, melting into

shall i have to undergo the Rite of Spring?

my loyalty belongs to Russian steppes and

snow,

but my true love lies entombed within a

jardin

the progeny between an artist and muse is art...

Jealousy
i want to feel all the lives behind closed doors
and take a polaroid snapshot of it
wanting to experience everything
without the consequences
from being everyone
*

your soul screams in poetry; yet your hands
cower in muteness
you would be writing novels; there's nothing
much to write about
how about conducting symphonies?; you're
deaf to harmonies
wanting to make music;
yet the soul cowards at the thought
natural at acting; you lack people skills
wanting to make children;
but you can't find a father

Faceted World

i'm a candle in the wind
reflecting multifacet worlds' lights
diamond without a king

i won't let them take you away from me
they can separate us like grain or sand

protect me like a little child
conjure your lullabies
spun from taffeta silk
cocooning me in your nonexistent embrace

the emptiness never left me
or the echos of foreign shores
sometimes it takes the bravest souls to fall

?

obsession (love?) is my concrete
that i use to fill the
yawning gap in my heart
yet when winter comes
ice slithers into our hole
spring rebriths potholes
freckling my heart
like weeds around the thorns:
i end up emptier than before
i poured you in as concrete
but you left as a crater

RUSSIA

an insatiable appetite for tragedy
i feel triggered listening to the rite of spring i
feel like i'm back in December and that there
should be snow falling outside and it feels like
the end of the year and everything is still
normal (as normal ever was) and there's
snowflakes whiling outside and there's a
Christmas tree downstairs and there's that
solemness to the end of the year and i'm
burning a candle that i usually only burn in fall
as i listen and this is one of those instances
where i feel scared of Russia. Although i'm not
scared of the dark when i look across the hall at
the open door to my parents room it seems like
a deep fathomless void where the boogie man
could pop out at any moment
there's a primal feel to the piece it contains the
aura that now surrounds Chernobyl and
Ukraine at the moment it is the primal fear
that awaits us when we are at the door to The

One and there is a final barrier between
understanding and mystery yet fear is the void
that spans it it is that Something that is
present within all cultures but that we are not
allowed to touch or name it is that aura that
has always existed since the dawn of time
it is the feeling of being haunted
i was so scared crossing the hall that if
someone came out of the shadows
unexpectedly i would scream and collapse
curling into a little ball like i am those 1950s
kids preparing for nuclear fallout and the low
flute and flurry of violins reminds me of
Russia's true nature or at least a part of him.
Winter is no longer my safe space
that's why i would love to visit Chernobyl, to
feel the lingering trace of the USSR, lingering
around like a god of death upon some
abandoned apartment wall

1917

Anastasia Beware Corrupt Duchesses Envying
Finite Glory. History Is Jealous, Killing Love,
Muzhiks, Nobility. Opulence...Polluted....Quits.

Rasputin Smiles, Triumphant Under Vodka
With
Xenophobia, Yawning *Zyma*

Being Bundga

For Dorethy Bundga, my grandmother

ya hochu kinja kawa[4]

coffee cups dance in the laminated kitchen

zyma's[5] heart can only warm us when

your green glass holding niagara's is your

emerald city's turned upside down

can you spell czechoslovakia where

hovena[6] is our fairy godmothers' fee for an

orient express to saint peter's? a

shoulder to cry on when

losing childhood to dreams.

our magic carpet's been

---

[4] I'd like a cup of coffee (Slovak)
[5] Winter (Russian)
[6] Shit (Slovak)

vandalized but your

Anastasia finally found her way to paris.

killing love is easier when people say your

influence was destructive but

all comes down to our love for steel skies

Тоска (Toska)

no it's not an Ichares complex

nor is it greed

we're suckers for martyr figures

you're my favorite masochist daydream

a little ball of clay

rolled around in your palm

the scent of lost memories,

You're on my mind again.

spinning on the

Wheel

spinning your flesh into

golden gauzy thread

embroidering into your storefront mannequin

Samovar

pregnant with honeyed

Чай,[7]

i nurture my imagination

within a tarnished

tummy, curved hips

suggestively poised

for hands to grasp

glowing golden,

my eastern european pride

shimmers across my

radiant lips,

poised to sprout

poetry from inside

my body

into faceted, iridescent

glasses that accessorize

tea from every angle,

humans savor the bittersweet

---

[7] Tea (Russian)

nectar of my soul,
unaware of which lover
impregnated my psyche
*

longing to break
my water so my
child can be born
through my sprout,
i can't let my ideas boil for
too long;
my frustration hisses,
breaking the peace of
a living room

Россия

A stone fairytale

conducted against a symphony of cyrillic

letters

waltzing in tsarist ballrooms to the

conversations of stuffy duchesses

their marble foundations forming words

resonating *vesna's* twirling sunflower petals

signaling *zyma's* buzzing blizzards to an end

its fluttery snowflakes falling to the ominous

tone

of His inevitable doom

in stone monasteries where wispy trails of

incense

from flickering flames hiss their dissidence

gregorian monks chant their requiem at

Russia's vigil

amidst the dying screams of russians

navigating their way through raging rivers of
bloodshed
His footsteps rage throughout the crunching,
tainted snow of History's blizzard
yet with open arms i wait for Him at History's
threshold
ready to welcome the elegant chaos that my
Russia is

how soon is siberia

i don't know if you're the devil masquerading

as love but

you'll only come back to haunt me

it's ok, you can (trust?)rest your madness in me

i can't deny the truth bleeding out from my

bones saying so

what if i'm your sacrifice?

i'll give kisses out on the scaffold

to any fucker doubting you

i'm the one with the scythe standing at the

crossroads of time

i ice skate back and forth over the Atlantic:

Fate tattooed in blood

the crescendo of centuries

contained within a symphony

i guess god is whatever you kill for

Russia III

Gatsby's green light disguised as
all the shades of a dying star
yeah i'm a rebel against living too
revolutionary spirit
i became broken and crazy to carry
your burden too

Vanya
i didn't cry when my grandfather died
my beatles nesting doll came from Boston
Prudential towering with luxury
fifteen you winked at me
and i was told your name was Ivan

i didn't cry when my grandmother died
post-covid Boston
your mother's stall lost at sea
amidst quincy market
complacent porcelain faces stared back at me

it was the bodiless dolls that
enticed me
disembodied porcelain under
a costume concealing invisibility
two came home with me

a fuschia matryoshka
beckoned me to
hand over more bens

and it was then that
your mother told me you died

i didn't cry-no-i lie
matryoshkas of grief spouted
from my eyes
Vanya i was going to return
that wink to you, flirt with you
at the wharf,
feet dangling over artificial ocean
red knitting in hand
watching british airways
land on governor's island

the tears kept unnesting
was it for you
your mother
this cruel war?
i don't know; tell me

EPILOGUE: Strange Hopes

lately I've been dreaming
about Neapolitan beaches
autumn isn't getting any younger
the charcoal smoke seems crisper
*

the winds roar, chanting of
of change
that's bounded by chains
Hope's a whore

before you dissolved into the mist
of memory
i remember how it felt feeling you within me
how the embers flickered
when your words made love to my soul

even now my dreams whisk you away to a
sacred place
where I can't even find solitude without
digging deeper
becoming sleepier

Acknowledgements

Firstly I must thank my parents, who have always lent their ears to my ranting poetic thoughts all these years. *Un grand merci* to Patrick Lawler and Linda Pennisi for being early proofreaders of select poems. I must thank Stephanie Duscher for her invaluable critique on this book's manuscript. Thank you to Francis at 100 covers for navigating me through the design process. Lastly, thank you to all the cultures that inspired me to write this and discover my body electric; *je vous aime.*